For Kathy and Bob

Living Together after Retirement

Graham Harrop

**Just pretend you're still driving
that big eighteen wheeler to Vermont.**

I didn't need a lifeguard BEFORE you retired, Roger, and I don't need one now!

It's just until I get used to you walking around the house in your underwear.

I just had to get out of the house
without him for awhile, Louise!

Is that big bad man at home all day
and scaring you? Well, we'll just
have to do something about that,
won't we? Won't we?

Let it go, Gregory, let it go...

**It's been two years since your
retirement party - you can take
your hat off now.**

Well, if you miss going to work in the mornings that much, get up and paint the house.

He's not used to you being
home all day...

Still struggling with with your post-retirement identity, Marvin?

There's a simple way to decide this.
You want to watch 'Ice Road Truckers'
and I want to watch 'Judge Judy'.
Judge Judy it is.

The good news is that we definitely didn't save too much for our retirement.

**Maybe you should phone the supermarket
and give them a heads-up
on these coupons!**

And when we see each other in the morning, it will be a nice surprise!

YOU STAY OUT OF THIS!

I thought since you used to work
on the road crew...

You can't sell half a house, Andrew!

**If you're not home by four,
that's wonderful!**

**Any other ideas for supplementing
our income besides inviting
Bill Gates to dinner?**

**You pumped up the tires on your
stationary bike half an hour ago!**

**For heaven's sake, Arthur - if you want
to go out - just GO out !**

You built Westminster Cathedral
YESTERDAY !

That's better!

**I'm sorry, but it drives me nuts
when you whistle through your nose!**

I'll tell you one thing - we wouldn't have
made it this far without you carrying
your end of the canoe, Ellen...

**Well, you're just going to have to
get your own decal, aren't you?**

**For the last time, the cat doesn't
NEED to go for a walk!**

I found you a part-time job.

The mail's not due for an hour!

**It hasn't been that easy for me,
either, Ralph!**

Same time tomorrow?

To order more copies of Living Together
After Retirement, please contact:
gtoonist@shaw.ca

29434463R00022

Printed in Great Britain
by Amazon